DEVoTIONAL PIANO

10 Piano Solos • Arranged by Don Phillips

MODERATE DIFFICULTY

Lillenas Publishing Co.
KANSAS CITY, MO. 64141

CONTENTS

O Love That Wilt Not Let Me Go

ALBERT L. PEACE
Arr. by Don Phillips

a tempo
Faster (♩ = 100)
Building gradually
Broader, "concerto" style
f

As before
Slowing
8va
mf
(8va)
8va
mp
p

O Jesus, I Have Promised

ARTHUR H. MANN
Arr. by Don Phillips

Tenderly (♩ = 76)

mp

A bit stronger

mf

rit.
a tempo

Gently
mp
rit.
rit.

God So Loved the World

JOHN STAINER
Arr. by Don Phillips

f
mp
mf
mp
rit.
p
As before

mp
mf
f
ff
accel.

Slowing
dim.
8va
8va
Freely
mp
rit.
Slowing to the end
8va
p
Ped

My Jesus, I Love Thee

ADONIRAM J. GORDON
Arr. by Don Phillips

As at first
rit.
mp
A little faster
mf
(bring out melody)
Gratefully
f

Quietly
ten.
ten.
ten.
ten.
Freely
rit.
l.h.
As at first
mp
8va

Beneath the Cross of Jesus

FREDERICK C. MAKER
Arr. by Don Phillips

With devotion

mp

Bring out melody

mf

rit.
a tempo
Gently
mp
mf

Freely
rit.
mp
Slowly
As at first
Ped.

O Divine Redeemer

CHARLES GOUNOD
Arr. by Don Phillips

mf
mp
mf
A little faster, with intensity
f

ff
rit.
Expressively (♩ = 84)
mf
Bring out melody

rit.

Stronger
a tempo
f
ff
Reverently, freely
mf
mp

Abide with Me

WILLIAM H. MONK
Arr. by Don Phillips

8va
As before
8va
(8va)
f
rit.
Gently (♩ = 84)
mp

A little faster (♩ = 88)
rit.
mf
Slower, freely
ten.
mf
ten.
ten.
mp
ten.
ten.
ten.
mf
a tempo
rit.
8va
mp

Near to the Heart of God

CLELAND McAFEE, with
new material by DON PHILLIPS
Arr. by Don Phillips

A little slower (♩ = 96)
rit.
bring out melody
As before
8va
(8va)
(8va)
rit.
a tempo

Stronger, a little faster
f
Broadening

8va
rit.
As before
mf
8va
(8va)
Slower
mp
rit.
8va
Slowly
8va
p

Something for Jesus

ROBERT LOWRY
Arr. by Don Phillips

Tenderly, freely *8va*

mp

rall.

mp

a tempo

p

mf

rit.
mp
A little stronger (♩= 76)
mf
Expansively
rit.
f
As before
rit.
mf
rit.
As at first
8va
mp
rit.
Ped

I Saw the Cross of Jesus

Anonymous
Arr. by Don Phillips

As at first
rit.
mp
In tempo (♩ = 72)
rit.
mf
Gently
mp
mel.
With quiet confidence

"Concerto"-like
f
rit.
Freely
mp
rit.
mf
mp
mp
rit.